Training
Peanut

by Debbie O'Brien

Editorial Offices: Glenview, Illinois • Parsippany, New Jersey • New York, New York
Sales Offices: Needham, Massachusetts • Duluth, Georgia • Glenview, Illinois
Coppell, Texas • Ontario, California • Mesa, Arizona

ISBN: 0-328-13300-0

6 7 8 9 10 V010 14 13 12 11 10 09 08 07

Tomás and Sofía wanted one thing more than anything else—they wanted to get a puppy. Every day they asked Mom about getting one.

"Cousin Luis has a puppy," declared Sofía, "and Luis is only six years old."

"Three of our neighbors have dogs. Our puppy would have plenty of playmates," Tomás said.

"Do you know how much work a puppy will be?" asked Mom. "You have to train a puppy. You have to feed it and walk it and bathe it."

"We know a puppy takes a lot of work, Mom!" exclaimed Tomás. "We'll help do all those things."

"I'll walk the puppy every day," promised Sofía, "even when it's raining!"

"And I'll feed the puppy," added Tomás. "I'll fill the puppy's dish once in the morning and again in the evening."

"I guess we can all help bathe the puppy," said Mom, as she started to smile. "What do you think? Is our family ready for a puppy?"

"Yes!" shouted Tomás and Sofía.

Mom laughed and said, "OK. You win. Let's get a puppy."

The family thought carefully about the kind of puppy they wanted. They finally decided to visit their neighbor, whose dog had just had five puppies. Sofía and Tomás picked out a tiny, soft, brown puppy. "This is the one we want, Mom," said Sofía. "What do you think?"

"I think she will be perfect for us," answered Mom, as she petted the new member of the household.

They took the puppy home and named her Peanut. Peanut was a very playful puppy. She loved to chase Tomás and Sofía. Sofía threw a ball and Peanut ran after it. Tomás got a toy rope and Peanut tugged at it.

When they tried to give her a bath in the tub, Peanut jumped around and splashed everyone. She leaped out of the tub and raced through the house dripping water everywhere!

Peanut was full of energy, and Peanut was also a little naughty. She ran outside and wouldn't come back when Tomás called her. She dug holes in Mrs. Vega's garden next door, which did not make Mrs. Vega very happy.

Peanut jumped up on every person who came through the door. She started chewing Mom's shoes, which did not make Mom very happy. Peanut pulled on the leash when Sofía walked her, and it almost looked like Peanut was walking Sofía!

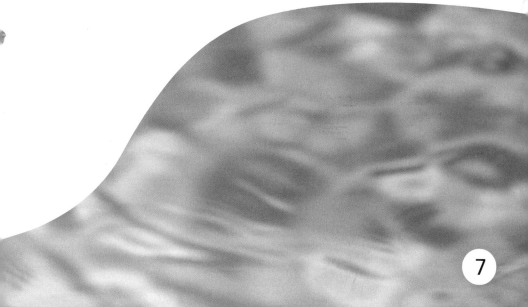

The family agreed that something had to be done about Peanut's behavior. The next day Mom came home with news.

"The community center is having a puppy training course. We can take Peanut there and the trainer will help us show Peanut how to obey," Mom said. She signed them up that day.

The next week, Mom, Tomás, and Sofía took Peanut to the community center. There they met Mr. Sanders, the puppy trainer, and four other puppies with their families. Everyone in the class wanted to help their puppies behave better.

Mr. Sanders began by showing the class how to give the *sit* command to a puppy.

"You must give the same command every time," Mr. Sanders explained. "Say the word *sit* just once, and make sure your puppy sits. Be sure to give your puppy plenty of praise when it obeys."

When Mr. Sanders asked everyone to practice the *sit* command with their puppies, Mom, Sofía, and Tomás took turns practicing with Peanut.

Peanut was more interested in jumping and playing with the other puppies than she was in sitting. The family knew it would take time before Peanut learned to sit on command. They knew they needed to be patient.

At the end of the class, Mr. Sanders assigned homework. He said, "I want you to practice the *sit* command every day with your puppy. You can give your puppy a small treat every time he or she obeys you."

All week, Tomás, Sofía, and Mom practiced the *sit* command with Peanut. Sometimes she would sit, and sometimes she would not. When Peanut obeyed, she would get a treat and a lot of praise.

"I think Peanut is starting to understand this," said Sofía, clapping her hands. "She just sat three times in a row!"

"I think Peanut is learning quickly," replied Mom, "but we still have to give her plenty of chances to practice."

During the second class, Mr. Sanders taught the puppies to sit and stay. He asked each family to give the puppies the *sit* command. Then he told them to step back and tell their puppy to stay. Some of the puppies got up and walked over to their families.

"That's OK," said Mr. Sanders. "This is a new command for the puppies, so it will take some time for them to learn what you want them to do."

At the end of the class, after the puppies had practiced their commands, Mr. Sanders let them play together. "The puppies have worked hard," he said. "They need some time to play and act like puppies."

"I think playtime is Peanut's favorite part of class!" whispered Tomás to Sofía.

In the next few weeks, Mr. Sanders taught the puppies how to *lie down* and *stay*. He taught them how to *heel*, or to walk beside the person holding their leash. All the puppies tugged at their leashes and tried to run ahead.

Mr. Sanders said, "It will take time for the puppies to learn the *heel* command. Take your puppies for lots of walks to practice."

One week, Mr. Sanders asked, "What problem behaviors do you have with your puppies?"

Problems

Jumping

Digging

As people spoke up, Tomás and Sofía realized that Peanut was not the only puppy who jumped on people or chewed shoes or dug holes. Mr. Sanders gave suggestions for fixing these problems.

He said, "Have a friend come to your home and ring the doorbell, but before you answer the door, ask your puppy to sit and stay. That will keep the puppy from jumping on your visitor. A bored puppy will dig holes, so don't forget to keep your puppy busy."

Barking

Chewing

One day, the class was held outside the community center. Tomás saw two teams playing soccer. The children on the teams seemed to be about his age, and they were having a lot of fun.

Tomás asked, "Mr. Sanders, who are those kids playing soccer?"

"That's the community center's team," Mr. Sanders replied. "If you're interested in joining, Tomás, the team is still looking for more players. In fact," he continued, "your family can look at the bulletin board in the lobby. The center has lots of activities for everyone."

Later, Tomás, Mom, and Sofía went to look at the list of the center's activities.

"Look, Mom," said Sofía. "Here's an art class I can take."

"And there is a computer course for adults," said Mom. "I have been meaning to learn how to use more programs on the computer."

Tomás chimed in, "Sofía, we can take swimming lessons this summer at the center's pool!"

At the end of the puppy training course, Mr. Sanders had a graduation party for the puppies. All the puppies had passed the course—even Peanut! Each puppy got a certificate and a bone.

"Remember to work with your puppies every day," said Mr. Sanders. "That way they will grow up to be well-behaved dogs. I hope to see you all next month for the advanced puppy training course!"

"We'll be back at the community center soon," said Sofía. "Peanut will get more training and I'll be taking the art class. Tomás will be playing soccer, and Mom will be learning about computers. We may take swimming lessons too!"

"Thanks to Peanut!" Tomás said. Peanut wagged her tail happily.

Service Dogs

    Service dogs are specially trained to help people with disabilities. These dogs may pull wheelchairs, open doors, flip light switches, or pick up things that have been dropped. Service dogs can alert people who cannot hear to sounds they need to know about, such as a knock at the door or a smoke alarm.

    The training process for service dogs begins with volunteers taking young puppies into their homes. The volunteers and their families help train the puppies and take the dogs to special training classes. When the puppies are a little more than a year old, they return to the training center for advanced training. They are then paired up with human partners and graduate as service dogs.